Blessed IN THE DARKNESS

JOURNAL

Also by Joel Osteen

Blessed IN THE DARKNESS

JOURNAL

How All Things Are Working for Your Good

#1 *New York Times* Bestselling Author

JOEL OSTEEN

FaithWords

NewYork • Nashville

FaithWords
Hachette Book Group
1290 Avenue of the Americas
New York, NY 10104
faithwords.com
twitter.com/faithwords

First Edition: October 2017

FaithWords is a division of Hachette Book Group, Inc.
The FaithWords name and logo are trademarks of Hachette Book Group, Inc.

The publisher is not responsible for websites (or their content) that are not owned by the publisher.

The Hachette Speakers Bureau provides a wide range of authors for speaking events. To find out more, go to www.hachettespeakersbureau.com or call (866) 376-6591.

Scripture quotations noted NIV are taken from *The Holy Bible, New International Version®* NIV®. Copyright © 1973, 1978, 1984, 2011 by Biblica, Inc.™ Used by permission. All rights reserved worldwide.

Scripture quotations noted NKJV are taken from the *New King James Version* of the Bible. Copyright © 1982 by Thomas Nelson, Inc. Used by permission. All rights reserved.

Scripture quotations noted NLT are taken from the *Holy Bible, New Living Translation,* copyright © 1996, 2004, 2007 by Tyndale House Foundation. Used by permission of Tyndale House Publishers, Inc., Carol Stream, IL 60188. All rights reserved.

Scripture quotations noted AMP are taken from *The Amplified Bible.* Copyright © 2015 by The Lockman Foundation, La Habra, CA 90631. All rights reserved. For permission to quote information visit www.lockman.org..

Scripture quotations noted AMPC are taken from *The Amplified Bible Classic Edition.* Copyright © 1954, 1958, 1962, 1964, 1965, 1987 by The Lockman Foundation, La Habra, CA 90631. All rights reserved. For permission to quote information visit www.lockman.org.

Scriptures noted TLB are taken from *The Living Bible,* copyright © 1971. Used by permission of Tyndale House Publishers, Inc., Carol Stream, IL 60188. All rights reserved.

Scriptures noted MSG are taken from *The Message.* Copyright © 1993, 1994, 1995, 1996, 2000, 2001, 2002. Used by permission of NavPress Publishing Group.

Scripture quotations noted ESV are taken from the *The Holy Bible, English Standard Version®.* Copyright © 2001 by Crossway, a publishing ministry of Good News Publishers. ESV® Text Edition: 2011. Used by permission. All rights reserved.

Scripture quotations noted KJV are from the *King James Version* of the Holy Bible.

Literary development: Lance Wubbels Literary Services, Bloomington, Minnesota.

ISBN: 978-1-5460-3277-9

Printed in the United States of America

10 9 8 7 6 5 4 3 2 1

Contents

. . . .

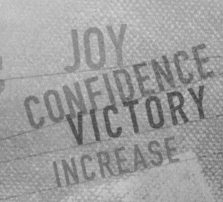

PERSEVERE
BELIEVE
GREATNESS
STRONG
BLESSED

CHARACTER
TRUST

JOY
CONFIDENCE
VICTORY
INCREASE

Introduction

. . . .

All of us will go through dark times that we don't understand, including loss, sickness, or divorce. Those experiences are a part of the human journey. But when we find ourselves in such difficult places, it's easy to get discouraged, give up on our dreams, and just settle.

That is why I wrote my book _Blessed in the Darkness_. We may not realize it, but when we feel buried in dark places, we are being blessed. God doesn't send the difficulties, but He will use those dark places to cause us to grow. We cannot reach our highest potential being in the light all the time. The dark places are all a part of His plan to make us into who we were created to be. That's where our character is developed. If we stay in faith and keep a good attitude when we go through challenges, we will not only grow, but we will see how God works all things together for our good.

This journal companion offers a practical tool that will help you harness insights from _Blessed in the Darkness_ and to focus on how to draw closer to God and trust Him when life doesn't make sense. It offers the same encouragement in daily doses supplemented by inspirational and thought-provoking material. You will find a wealth of scriptures, inspirational quotations, selected stories, prayers, and points for contemplation. All are provided to engage you in a process of reflection that will enhance your faith and help you to rise to a new level of being your best.

The thoughts and questions addressed in the following pages will help you to understand that there are seeds of talent, potential, and greatness buried deep within you that will only come to life in the darkness. As you learn to trust Him when life doesn't make sense, it's just a matter of time before you break out and blossom into your full potential.

I am delighted in your interest in this journal. It shows that you want to put your faith into action and reach the highest level of your destiny, and God loves that. You'll learn that if you will go through the dark place in the valley trusting, believing, and knowing that God is still in control, you will come to the table that is already prepared for you, where your cup runs over.

This journal is an open door to self-discovery, so step through and begin the journey toward living the life you were born to live. My prayer is that you will take some time each day to read the entries and to add your own thoughts. But don't rush through it. Slow yourself down and take the time to reflect on your life. Let the scriptures speak to your heart. If you are facing challenges or barriers, there are prayers and inspirational quotes to help remind you that God is with you each and every moment. Be still and listen to what God is saying through these words, then put words to your responses.

This is a journal to record life lessons that you don't want to forget. It could be the start to a brand-new beginning for you. Underline important ideas within these pages, write yourself notes of encouragement in the margins as you read, and jot down fresh ideas that come to you as you read. Especially seek God's help and guidance regarding areas in which He may want to change you. It's a reflection of your life journey. What you record you remember. You will discover that it will bring clarity to what God has done, is doing, and wants to do in your life.

Journaling has also been shown to improve problem-solving abilities. Many people find that using a journal helps them to better assess their thoughts and feelings and to find clarity. The process of putting pen to paper and then seeing your words on the page can help you solve problems while keeping matters in perspective and priorities straight. You may release pent-up emotions in the process, and that is a good thing too.

Be as honest as possible as you write your responses. Don't be afraid to freely express your thoughts and feelings. Don't worry about punctuation, spelling, or grammar when making your own entries. You won't be graded on this.

This journal is designed to provide you eighteen days of daily inspiration and encouragement in your walk of faith. It is best to read day to day in a quiet place where you can meditate and contemplate for brief periods, away from the usual distractions. Take your time and enter your thoughts and encouragements. Once you've gone through it, feel free to begin again. Replenish your spirit and listen for the still, small voice of God's grace and direction.

Let this journal serve as a record of your daily progress and your entries as a testimony of your faith. Enjoy the process as you uncover the keys to finding light in the darkness and becoming the person of faith and character God designed you to be, even when hope seems impossible.

CHARACTER
TRUST

JOY
CONFIDENCE
VICTORY
INCREASE

PERSEVERE
BELIEVE
GR
STRONG
BLESSED

Blessed in the Dark Places

CHAPTER ONE

Key Truth

All of us at some point will go through a dark place—a <u>sickness, a divorce, a loss.</u> It's easy to wonder where the blessings are when we go through things we don't understand. But God uses the <u>dark places as a part of His divine plan.</u> <u>We can gain blessings in times of darkness</u> <u>that we cannot gain in the light.</u>

Throughout the Scripture, every person who did something great went through dark places. Moses made a mistake and killed an Egyptian man. He spent forty lonely years on the back side of the desert, feeling as though he had blown it. But in that dark place he was being prepared, developing patience, humility, strength, and trust. Without the dark place Moses would never have led the Israelites out of slavery and toward the Promised Land. The dark place was a prerequisite for his stepping into the fullness of his destiny, and it's a prerequisite for us as well. Esther was an orphan, having lost both of her parents, and living in a foreign country. She felt alone, forsaken, abandoned, in a dark place. Yet God used her to help save the people of Israel. Elijah descended from a great mountain victory into a dark place of depression so low that he wanted to die, yet he's one of the heroes of faith. When Joseph was falsely accused and put in prison for thirteen years, the Scripture says, "He was laid in chains of iron, *and* his soul entered into the iron" (Ps. 105:18 AMPC). In that prison Joseph developed strength, a perseverance that he could not have gotten any other way.

There are some lessons you can only learn in the dark places. It's in the dark places that you really grow. They're where your character is developed, where you learn to trust God and to persevere, and where your spiritual muscles are made strong. In the dark places you pray more, you draw closer to God, and you take time to get quiet and listen to what He's saying. In those dark places you reevaluate your priorities, you slow down and take time for family, and you get a new appreciation for what God has given you.

Quit complaining about the difficulties you're going through, about how unfair it is, about who did you wrong. It may be uncomfortable, you may not like it, but it's working for your good. You're getting stronger; it's developing something in you that you can only get in the dark. You can't reach your highest potential being in the light all the time. To have no opposition, no problems, and nobody coming against you may sound good, but it will stunt your growth.

Jesus said, "Unless a kernel of wheat is planted in the soil and dies, it remains alone. But its death will produce many new kernels" (John 12:24 NLT). A seed's potential will never be released until it's been planted and goes through the process of germination—the outer shell breaks off and the new growth begins. That's when it will blossom and bring forth much fruit. The problem with many people is that they want the fruit, but they don't want to go through the process of being planted in the dark soil and something dying so that God can birth something new.

My challenge is for you to be willing to go through the process. Dare to trust Him. He knows what He's doing. He doesn't send the difficulty, but He will use it. Don't fight the dark places. There may be dirt all around you, it's uncomfortable, but that dirt is not there to stop you. It's there to bring out the greatness on the inside.

>> Consider This <<

King David said, "I called on the LORD in distress; the LORD
answered me *and* set me in a broad place" (Ps. 118:5 NKJV). He
didn't get enlarged in the good times; he was enlarged when things
weren't going his way. What shaped him into a champion?
What is God using to shape your life?

....

....

....

....

....

....

....

....

....

....

....

....

....

....

....

....

....

....

>> **What the Scriptures Say** <<

Even though I walk through the darkest valley, I will fear no evil,
for you are with me; your rod and your staff, they comfort me.
You prepare a table before me in the presence of my enemies.
You anoint my head with oil; my cup overflows.

Psalm 23:4–5 NIV

Who among you fears the LORD and obeys his servant?
If you are walking in darkness, without a ray of light,
trust in the LORD and rely on your God.

Isaiah 50:10 NLT

....

....

....

....

....

....

....

....

....

....

....

....

....

....

....

>> Thoughts for Today <<

It is in the deepest darkness of the starless midnight that
men learn how to hold on to the hidden Hand most tightly
and how that Hand holds them; that He sees where we do not,
and knows the way He takes; and though the way be to
us a roundabout way, it is the right way.

A. T. Pierson

Every life has dark tracks and long stretches of somber tint,
and no representation is true to fact that dips its pencil only
in light, and flings no shadows on the canvas.

Alexander Maclaren

When a train goes through a tunnel and it gets dark,
you don't throw away the ticket and jump off.
You sit still and trust the engineer.

Corrie ten Boom

....

....

....

....

....

....

....

....

....

....

>> A Prayer for Today <<

Father, thank You that just as You lead me to green pastures
and still waters, so You lead me through the dark valleys. I believe
that You bless me even in the dark places and that what's meant
for my harm is going to work to my advantage. Thank You that
I can put my trust in You, that You are in control, and know
that You are preparing a table for me, bringing me into a fresh
anointing and into increase to where my cup runs over.
I believe that You have an exclamation point waiting
for me. In Jesus' Name. Amen.

Takeaway Truth

Think about this: an exclamation point is simply a question mark straightened out. If you want God to turn your question marks, the things you don't understand, into exclamation points, you have to trust Him. In those dark places where it isn't fair, dare to say, "God, I know You're still on the throne. I may not understand this valley I'm in, but I know that on the other side is my exclamation point."

PERSEVERE
BELIEVE
GREATNESS
STRONG
BLESSED

CHARACTER
TRUST

JOY
CONFIDENCE
VICTORY
INCREASE

Night Seasons

CHAPTER TWO

Key Truth

There are times in all our lives when we're praying and believing, but we feel alone, forgotten, as though our situation is never going to change. It's a night season. It doesn't look as though anything is happening, but God is working behind the scenes. He does His greatest work in the dark. He hasn't forgotten about us.

Blessed
IN
THE DARKNESS

. . . .

n the night seasons, when life feels unfair, things aren't going
your way, and you don't see anything happening, you have
to remind yourself that God is still in control. Just because
you don't see anything happening doesn't mean that God is
not working.

As a young man, David defeated Goliath. It was a great
victory. But after that he spent years running from King Saul,
hiding in caves, sleeping in the desert. I'm sure he prayed,
"God, deliver me from Saul. This is unfair." But it was as though
the heavens were silent. God didn't change the night season,
which is a time of testing and proving. We can either choose to
get negative and live discouraged, or we can choose to say, "God,
I don't understand it. It's not fair, but I trust in You. I know
You're not just the God of the daytime, but also the God of the
night seasons."

In the Scripture, Ruth lost her husband at an early age
(see Ruth 1). She was devastated, heartbroken. She could have
given up on life and lived in self-pity. But she understood this
principle: the night seasons are not the end. The bad breaks, the
disappointments, and the losses are simply additional steps on
the way to your destiny.

The psalmist said, "Weeping may endure for a night, but
joy comes in the morning" (Ps. 30:5 NKJV). Your story doesn't
end in the night. The night is temporary. Sickness is temporary.
Loneliness is temporary. An addiction is temporary. Ruth went
on to fall in love with another man, got married, and had a baby.
Her story didn't end in the dark.

When things aren't working out and you feel as though you're going in the wrong direction, don't get discouraged because God has not changed it yet. It's just a night season. It's not permanent. It's not how your story ends. You may not see anything happening, but God is at work. Dare to trust Him. Keep moving forward in faith, keep believing. It's just a matter of time before the morning breaks forth.

You've heard the phrase *the night shift*. It refers to people who work during the night, but think of it another way. In the night, things are going to shift. The Scripture says, "God never sleeps." He doesn't just work the night shift, He shifts things in the night. You may be in a night season, and you may not see how the difficulties you face can work out. Don't worry—a night shift is coming. The God who works the night shift is going to shift things in your favor. There's going to be a shift in your health, a shift in your finances, a shift with that addiction. You think you're going to have it for years. It looks permanent. No, get ready for a night shift.

Things may look permanent in your life—the sickness, the panic attacks, the lack and struggle. Thoughts will tell you, *You'll always have to deal with that.* Don't believe those lies. You're in a night season, which means you're in perfect position for a night shift. God specializes in shifting things in the dark. Instead of worrying, all through the day say, "Lord, thank You for a night shift. Thank You that things are changing in my favor. It's dark now, but I believe what You said. Light is about to come bursting in."

>> Consider This <<

When a caterpillar is in the dark confinement of the cocoon,
it doesn't realize it is undergoing a transformation into a beautiful
butterfly. Similarly, we all dislike the night seasons, but it is in
the dark that a transformation is taking place within us.
How have night seasons transformed your life?

*It has kept me calm serene and keept
me to solitude
*It has allowed me to appreciate me more
knowing that keeping alone at times is to
my advantage it keeps and give me peace
* It has builer my patience and contentment

>> **What the Scriptures Say** <<

When darkness overtakes [the righteous],
light will come bursting in.

Psalm 112:4 TLB

And let us not grow weary while doing good, for in due season
we shall reap if we do not lose heart.

Galatians 6:9 NKJV

....
....
....
....
....
....
....
....
....
....
....
....
....
....
....
....
....
....
....

>> **Thoughts for Today** <<

Having the answers is not essential to living. What is essential is the sense of God's presence during dark seasons of questioning.

Ravi Zacharias

In the darkest of nights cling to the assurance that God loves you, that He always has…a path that you can tread and a solution to your problem—and you will experience that which you believe. God never disappoints anyone who places his trust in Him.

Basilea Schlink

The next time you find yourself alone in a dark alley facing the undeniables of life, don't cover them with a blanket or ignore them with a nervous grin. Don't turn up the TV and pretend they aren't there. Instead, stand still, whisper His name, and listen. He is nearer than you think.

Max Lucado

....

....

....

....

....

....

....

....

....

....

....

>> A Prayer for Today <<

Father in heaven, thank You that You are the God of hard places,
the God of lonely times, and the God of night seasons. I believe
that no matter what comes my way, it's not a surprise to You,
and You still have me in the palms of Your hands. Thank You that
You always have a solution, and that breakthroughs are headed
my way. Thank You that You turn mourning to dancing,
sorrow to joy, sickness to health, lack to abundance. I believe
that all is well, and though it may be night now,
morning is coming. In Jesus' Name. Amen.

Takeaway Truth

In the night seasons, you need to pass the tests, change where you need to change, and deal with the areas that God is bringing to light. Then, because your character has been developed, God will bring you out of that night season and get you to where you're supposed to be. But we can only develop some things in the dark. Without the night seasons, we wouldn't become all God created us to be.

CONFIDENCE
VICTORY
INCREASE

CHARACTER
TRUST

PERSEVERE
BELIEVE
GREATNESS
STRONG
BLESSED

Secret Frustrations

CHAPTER THREE

Key Truth

Life is full of seeming contradictions that try to
keep us in the darkness. All of us have secret
frustrations—things that we know God could
change. He could open the door, or remove the
temptation, or give us the baby we're dreaming
about, but it's not happening. It's easy to get
stuck with the "why" questions.

Blessed
IN THE DARKNESS

God used the apostle Paul in a great way, but, as effective as Paul was, he had a secret frustration. He called it "a thorn in the flesh." Scholars have debated whether it was a physical condition such as an illness, an emotional issue, the persecution he often endured, or the people who were constantly coming against him. Whatever that thorn was, whatever was bothering him, Paul prayed three times for God to remove it. One translation of the Scripture says he "implored" God to take it away. That means that Paul gave it his best argument. "God, I've served You. I've been my best. I've prayed for others, and they've been healed. God, please heal me. I'm tired of this thorn, and I'm tired of people treating me wrongly because of it. God, please take it away." If anybody ever had pull with God, it was Paul. But what's interesting is that God never removed that thorn. Paul wrote in 2 Corinthians 12 that God's answer to him was, "My grace is sufficient for you. My power shows up greatest in weakness."

Is there something you've implored God to change, perhaps a situation in your health, your finances, a relationship? You've asked again and again, but nothing's improved. I'm not saying to give up and settle there in a dark place. What I'm saying is that if God is not removing it or changing it, don't let it steal your joy, don't let it sour your life. God has given you the grace to be there. The right attitude is, *I'm not going to let this secret frustration frustrate me anymore. God, I know Your grace is sufficient for me. I have the power to be here with a good attitude. I believe that at the right time You will change it; but if it never changes, I'm still going to be my best and honor You.*

You have to make up your mind about what frustrates you. If that issue with your spouse doesn't change, if your health doesn't improve, if you have to put up with that grouchy boss for the rest of your life, if you have to struggle with that temptation till the day you die, you're not going to complain, and you're not going to use it as an excuse to slack off. You're going to tap into this grace. It's sufficient for you. That means you are well able to enjoy your life in spite of the secret frustrations.

Here's a key: don't focus on the frustration. Paul could have gone around thinking, *God, why won't You remove this thorn?* If he had gotten stuck on the whys of life, he would have never fulfilled his destiny. We do the same when we keep asking why God hasn't changed our child or caused our business to grow. Faith is trusting God when life doesn't make sense.

If you're going to reach your full potential, you can't be a weakling. You have to be a warrior. There will be things you don't understand, things that don't make sense, but God knows what He's doing. His ways are better than our ways. His thoughts are higher than our thoughts. He is the Potter, and we are the clay. If it's supposed to be removed, He'll remove it. If not, dig your heels in and fight the good fight of faith. You have the grace you need for every situation.

>> Consider This <<

God did not remove Paul's thorn in the flesh nor did He touch Moses' tongue and take away the stuttering. Whatever your secret frustration is, whether an imperfection or thorn, what is God saying to you about it?

>> **What the Scriptures Say** <<

"Behold, I have refined you, but not as silver; I have tested you in the furnace of affliction."

Isaiah 48:10 NKJV

"Look, I go forward, but He is not *there,* and backward, but I cannot perceive Him; when He works on the left hand, I cannot behold *Him*; when He turns to the right hand, I cannot see *Him*. But He knows the way that I take; *when* He has tested me, I shall come forth as gold."

Job 23:8–10 NKJV

>> Thoughts for Today <<

St. Paul was tempted to think that he could do far better work
for his beloved Master if only that "thorn" could be removed.
But God knew that Paul would be a better man
with the "thorn" than without it.

Author Unknown

What then are we to do about our problems? We must
learn to live with them until such time as God delivers us
from them. We must pray for grace to endure them without
murmuring. Problems patiently endured will work for
our spiritual perfecting. They harm us only when we
resist them or endure them unwillingly.

A. W. Tozer

Regardless the depth of one's pain, God promises His grace is
always sufficient to meet the need to continue a Christian life
of joy, peace, hope, service, contentment, faith, and worship
despite the circumstances being unchanged.

Randy Smith

....

....

....

....

....

....

....

....

....

>> **A Prayer for Today** <<

Father, thank You that even when I don't understand why
something isn't changing, even when it seems unfair, Your grace
is sufficient for every situation. I'm going to keep trusting You and
not let this secret frustration keep me from my destiny. You know
what You're doing, and I'm going to keep moving forward by
grace in spite of my weakness and what's coming against me.
I believe that even if the situation never changes, my character
is being developed and that secret frustration is going to give
way to a huge blessing. In Jesus' Name. Amen.

Takeaway Truth

Don't let secret frustrations steal your joy and keep you in a dark place. Have a new perspective. You have the grace for anything you're facing. If God is not removing it, don't try to figure it out; trust Him. You will not only enjoy your life more, but God will remove everything that's supposed to be removed, and you will rise higher, overcome obstacles, and become everything you were created to be.

JOY
CONFIDENCE
VICTORY
INCREASE

PERSEVERE
BELIEVE
GREATNESS
STRONG
BLESSED

CHARACTER
TRUST

Unconditional Trust

CHAPTER FOUR

Key Truth

When our prayers aren't being answered
and things aren't going our way, too often we
condition our trust and say, "God, if You answer
my prayers in the way I want, I'll be my best."
The problem is that there will always be things
we don't understand. Faith is trusting God
when life doesn't make sense.

t's easy to trust God when things are going our way and life is good. But when the problem isn't turning around and we're not seeing favor, too often we get discouraged and condition our trust, thinking that when God finally answers our prayers in the way we want and according to our timetable, we'll have a good attitude. The problem with conditional trust is that there will always be something that doesn't work out the way we want. The question is, are you mature enough to accept God's answers even when they're not what you were hoping for?

This is what three Hebrew teenagers did in the Scripture. They wouldn't bow down to the king of Babylon's golden idol. He was so furious that he was about to have them thrown into a fiery furnace. They said, "King, we're not worried. We know that our God will deliver us. But even if He doesn't, we're still not going to bow down." That's unconditional trust. It's saying, "I believe God's going to turn this situation around, but even if He doesn't, I'm still going to be happy. I know that God is still on the throne. If He's not changing it, He has a reason. My life is in His hands."

Dare to trust Him not just when things are going your way, but even when you don't understand it. The psalmist said, "The LORD will work out his plans for my life" (Ps. 138:8 NLT). You don't have to work it all out. You don't have to make it happen in your own strength, try to manipulate people, or fight all your battles alone. Why don't you relax and take the pressure off yourself and let God work out His plan for your life? He can do it better than you can. He knows the best path. That's what the Hebrew teenagers were saying. "We know God will deliver us from this fire. But even if He doesn't, we're not going to get upset and start panicking. The Most High God, the Creator of the universe, is working out His plan for our lives." All the forces of darkness cannot stop what God has ordained. Sickness can't stop Him. Trouble at work can't stop Him. Disappointments and setbacks can't stop Him.

You may have a lot coming against you. You feel as though you're about to be thrown into a fire. The good news is, you're not going to go in there alone. You can't be put in that fire unless God allows it. God is working out His plan. Sometimes His plan includes fiery furnaces. Sometimes it includes giants, Red Seas, Pharaohs, and other people who don't like you. Sometimes obstacles will seem insurmountable. You don't see a way, but, like those teenagers, you have unconditional trust. "I know God will deliver me, but even if He doesn't, I'm still going to have a song of praise. I'm still going to have an attitude of faith. I'm still going to live my life happy."

The king had these teenagers thrown into the fiery furnace. The fire was so hot that when the guards opened the door, they were instantly killed. In a few minutes, the king came to check on them. He looked into the furnace and couldn't believe his eyes. He said, "Didn't we throw in three bound men? I see four men loosed, and one looks like the Son of God." What was that? God working out His plan for their lives!

>> Consider This <<

The loss of my father was the darkest hour of my life. But as was true in my life, God's plan for your life is bigger than your plan. But it may not happen the way you think. God doesn't take us in a straight line. There will be twists, turns, disappointments, losses, and bad breaks. How have you responded to these dark times when God doesn't seem to be answering your prayers? How can you keep these issues where a "want" is not being fulfilled from consuming your thoughts and prayers?

>> **What the Scriptures Say** <<

"For my thoughts are not your thoughts, neither are your ways
my ways," declares the Lord. "As the heavens are higher than
the earth, so are my ways higher than your ways and
my thoughts than your thoughts."

Isaiah 55:8–9 NIV

Trust God from the bottom of your heart; don't try to figure
out everything on your own. Listen for God's voice in
everything you do, everywhere you go; he's the one
who will keep you on track.

Proverbs 3:5–6 MSG

....

....

....

....

....

....

....

....

....

....

....

....

....

....

>> **Thoughts for Today** <<

We cannot always trace God's hand, but we can
always trust God's heart.

Charles Spurgeon

What does a child do whose mother or father allows something
to be done that it cannot understand? There is only one
way to peace. The loving child trusts.

Amy Carmichael

Never be afraid to trust an unknown future to a known God.

Corrie ten Boom

>> **A Prayer for Today** <<

Father in heaven, there are many things in my life that I don't understand, things I want to see changed, and new doors that I want to see open, but if they never happen, I'm still going to trust You. Thank You for giving me the grace to be happy today, and I gladly leave these matters in Your hands. I believe that as long as I keep honoring You and being my best, at the right time You will get me to where I'm supposed to be. I trust that You will not only give me the desires of my heart, but You'll do more than I ask or think. In Jesus' Name. Amen.

Takeaway Truth

The closed doors, the disappointments,
the delays—it's all working for you. If God's
not changing it, not removing it, not opening
it, don't fight it. Learn to embrace where you
are. He's given you the grace not just to be
there but to be there with a good attitude.
If you're going to pass the test, keep a smile
on your face. Keep a song in your heart.
Keep passion in your spirit. He's working
out His plan for your life.

PERSEVERE
BELIEVE
GREATNESS
STRONG
BLESSED

JOY
CONFIDENCE
VICTORY
INCREASE
CHARACTER
TRUST

Don't Waste Your Pain

CHAPTER FIVE

Key Truth

We all go through difficulties, setbacks, and loss. Pain is a part of life, and it often feels like a dark place. It's easy to think, *God, why did this happen to me?* But one of the most important things I've learned is not to put a question mark where God has put a period. The key is what you do in your times of pain.

Blessed
IN THE DARKNESS

Sometimes we look at the pieces in our lives that don't make sense—the loss of a loved one, a divorce, a bout with cancer—and think these couldn't be a part of God's plan. You have to trust that even in the painful times when you're hurting, you're lonely, and you're undergoing medical treatment, God doesn't make any mistakes. He's already designed your life down to the smallest detail. God didn't promise that there wouldn't be any pain, suffering, or disappointment. But He did promise that it would all work out for our good. That piece that's painful, that doesn't look as though it makes sense—when everything comes together, it's going to fit perfectly in place.

The key is what you do in your times of pain. Pain will change us. Difficulties, heartache, suffering—they don't leave us the same. When I went through the loss of my father, I didn't come out of that experience the same person. I was changed. If you go through a divorce or a legal battle, eventually the experience will pass and you will get through it, but you will be different. How the pain changes you is up to you. You can come out bitter, or you can come out better. You can come out defeated, having given up on your dreams, or you can come out with a greater trust in God and blessed with a new fire, looking for new opportunities in front of you.

We all experience pain. My challenge is, don't just go through it; grow through it. That difficulty is an opportunity to get stronger, to develop character, to gain a greater trust in God. Anybody can fall apart; anybody can get bitter—that's easy. But what that's doing is wasting your pain.

Sometimes we bring the pain on ourselves. We make poor choices, get into a relationship that we knew would not be good, or get in over our head in our spending, and then there's the pain—we're dealing with the consequences. God is full of mercy, and He'll always give us the grace to get through it. But in order not to waste the pain, you have to learn the lesson in that pain. Don't be a hardhead and keep going through the same pain again and again.

There are times when God will allow us to go through a painful season so He can birth something new on the inside. The apostle Paul said, "The God of all comfort, who comforts us in all our troubles, so that we can comfort those in any trouble with the comfort we ourselves receive from God" (2 Cor. 1:3–4 NIV). If you go through something you don't understand, instead of getting upset have a new perspective. God allowed this to happen because He trusts you. He knows He can count on you to take the same comfort, the same healing, the same encouragement that helped you overcome this trouble, and share it with others.

The Scripture says, "Because of the joy awaiting [Jesus], he endured the cross" (Heb. 12:2 NLT). Have that attitude when you experience pain, and you're going to come out refined, purified, prepared, and stronger. That pain is not there to stop you; it's there to develop you, to prepare you, to increase you.

>> **Consider This** <<

Candy Lightner took one of life's greatest pains, the death
of her daughter, and turned it around to become a force for
good through the founding of Mothers Against Drunk Driving.
Most of us are not going to experience something that tragic,
but when you've been through something, in one sense
you've been given a gift. You're uniquely qualified to help
somebody else in that situation. What have you gone
through that you could use to help others?

>> **What the Scriptures Say** <<

And not only *this*, but [with joy] let us exult in our sufferings *and* rejoice in our hardships, knowing that hardship (distress, pressure, trouble) produces patient endurance; and endurance, proven character (spiritual maturity); and proven character, hope *and* confident assurance [of eternal salvation].

Romans 5:3–4 AMP

You know we call those blessed [happy, spiritually prosperous, favored by God] who were steadfast *and* endured [difficult circumstances]. You have heard of the *patient* endurance of Job and you have seen the Lord's outcome [how He richly blessed Job]. The Lord is full of compassion and is merciful.

James 5:11 AMP

>> **Thoughts for Today** <<

God, who foresaw your tribulation, has specially armed you
to go through it, not without pain but without stain.

C. S. Lewis

Don't waste your pain; use it to help others.

Rick Warren

How many moments of pain are wasted because we never
sat still enough to learn from them?

Kevin DeYoung

....

....

....

....

....

....

....

....

....

....

....

....

....

....

>> **A Prayer for Today** <<

Father, thank You that You're not only in control of my life, but You're in control of the enemy. I believe that whatever pain comes my way is completely controlled by You and that You will only allow what I can handle and what will be for my good. Thank You that there is a purpose in my pain, whether I understand it or not, and that You are not only going to bring me out stronger, increased, and promoted, but You're going to use me to help others who are struggling in that same area. In Jesus' Name. Amen.

Takeaway Truth

Difficulties will come, and pain is a part of life, so don't get discouraged. In the tough dark times, God is getting you prepared. He's getting you ready to receive blessings, favor, and increase as you've never seen. Don't just go through it, grow through it. If you'll do this, your pain is going to be turned into your gain. Out of that pain you're going to give birth to a new level of your destiny.

CONFIDENCE
VICTORY
INCREASE

PERSEVERE
BELIEVE
GREATNESS
STRONG
BLESSED

CHARACTER
TRUST

Blessed by Your Enemies

CHAPTER SIX

Key Truth

Goliath was strategically placed in David's path—
not to defeat him, but to promote him. Without
Goliath, David would have never taken the throne.
In the same way, God has ordained Goliaths to
come across your path—not to stop you, but to
establish you. It's all a part of God's plan to get
you to where you're supposed to be.

We all know that God can bless us, show us favor, promote us, heal us. But what we don't always realize is that God can use our enemies to bless us. What you think is a disappointment someone has caused—that person who left you, that coworker who's trying to make you look bad, that friend who betrayed you—you may not like it, but you couldn't reach your destiny without it.

If it weren't for Goliath, David would be known only as a shepherd boy. Goliath was created for David's purpose. Part of his destiny was to establish who David was. What may have looked like a setback for David was really a setup to get him to the throne. In the same way, God has lined up divine connections, people who will be good to you and push you forward, and people who will try to stop you and discourage you. If you don't understand this principle, you'll get discouraged and think, *God, why is this happening to me?* That opposition is not there to stop you; it's there to establish you. When you overcome, not only will you step up to a new level of your destiny, but everyone around you will see the favor of God on your life.

In 2002 we received word that the city leaders were thinking about selling the Compaq Center. When I heard this news, something came alive inside me. I knew that building was supposed to be ours. When word got out in the city that we were interested in it, the opposition began. In particular, one local high-powered businessman strongly opposed our buying it and said sarcastically, "It will be a cold day in hell before Lakewood gets that building." As it turned out, that executive was one of those Goliaths whom God strategically places in our path.

When I heard how much he was against us, something rose up inside me. I had been determined before, but now there was a holy determination. I had a new fire, a new passion, a new resolve. Every time things got tough and I was tempted to think it wasn't going to work out, I would recall his words, *a cold day in hell*, and instantly get my passion back. Sometimes God will put an enemy in your life to keep you stirred up.

David said to God, "You prepare a table before me in the presence of my enemies" (Ps. 23:5 NIV). When God brings you through the dark valley of opposition, He's going to do it in such a way that all your enemies can see He has blessed you. Our building is on the second busiest freeway in the nation. Every time that executive who said we'd never get the Compaq Center drives by, I imagine he thinks, *It's a cold day in hell.*

You may be up against a similar enemy right now—an enemy to your health, your finances, a relationship. It may look as though it's never going to work out. Have this new perspective: God is preparing the table right now for you as He did for David, as He did for us, where not just all your friends can see it, but even your enemies—the doubters, the critics, the people who said it wouldn't work out—are going to see you blessed, healed, promoted, vindicated, in a position of honor and influence.

>> **Consider This** <<

Has God placed a Goliath in your path in the past to stir you
up and overcome a challenge? Are you up against opposition
at this present time? What is your perspective of it?
How aligned are your thoughts to David's statement
that God is preparing a table for you?

....

....

....

....

....

....

....

....

....

....

....

....

....

....

....

....

....

>> **What the Scriptures Say** <<

Don't be intimidated in any way by your enemies.

They set taskmasters over [the people of Israel] to afflict
them with their burdens.... But the more they afflicted them,
the more they multiplied and grew.

>> Thoughts for Today <<

When God gives a promise, He always tries our faith. Just as
the roots of trees take firmer hold when they are contending
with the wind, so faith takes a firmer hold when it
struggles with adverse appearances.

Robert Murray McCheyne

When by the malice of enemies God's people are brought
to greatest troubles, there is deliverance near to be sent
from God to them.

David Dickson

Adversity is not simply a tool. It is God's most effective tool for
the advancement of our spiritual lives. The circumstances and
events that we see as setbacks are oftentimes the very things that
launch us into periods of intense spiritual growth.

Charles Stanley

....

....

....

....

....

....

....

....

....

....

....

>> **A Prayer for Today** <<

Father in heaven, thank You for my friends, and thank You for my enemies as well. Thank You that I don't have to be intimidated by what somebody says or does, or by a sickness or by how big an obstacle is. I am not weak or lacking in any good thing, and I know that the pressure that I am under cannot stop me and is going to increase me. I believe that I am more than a conqueror because You are on my side. I look forward to how You will use my enemies to bless me and help me reach my highest potential. In Jesus' Name. Amen.

Takeaway Truth

You need to see every enemy, every adversity, every disappointment in a new light: the opposition is not there to defeat you, it's there to increase you, to make you better. Those people who try to push you down, the betrayal, the disappointment— none of these can keep you from your destiny. God has the final say. If you keep the right attitude, God will even use the opposition to bless you.

CHARACTER
TRUST
JOY
CONFIDENCE
VICTORY
INCREASE

PERSEVERE
BELIEVE
GREATNESS
STRONG
BLESSED

It's All
Good

CHAPTER SEVEN

Key Truth

Life is full of things that we see as being
negative and bad. But God will use everything
that happens in your life—the closed doors,
the delays, the person who did you wrong—
to push you further into your destiny. God says,
"It's all good. If you'll trust Me, I'm going
to use it for your good."

We're not going to understand everything that happens and doesn't happen in our lives. If you try to figure it all out, you'll get frustrated. God can see the big picture for our lives. He knows where the dead ends are, the shortcuts, the bumpy roads that are going to cause you heartache and pain. He'll keep doors closed that you prayed would open, because He knows going through them would be a waste of your time. When you're mature, instead of getting bitter when things don't work out, you'll say, "God, I trust You. I may not like it, but I believe You know what's best for me."

Some of the things that God has in your future you wouldn't be able to handle if He gave them to you right now. He loves you too much to let that happen. He's developing your character, growing you up. That boss who gets on your nerves—you keep trying to pray him away. The reason he's not going away is that God is using him like sandpaper to rub the rough edges off you. As you keep doing the right thing, keeping your mouth closed, being respectful, being faithful to your responsibilities, that's doing a work in you. You couldn't develop your character without him. You may not like it, but it's good.

Why don't you quit fighting everything you don't like and have this new perspective: it's all good? You can say, "I don't like how this has gone, but God is on the throne, and He's in control of my life. This thing that has come against me may have been meant to harm me, but He promised He would use it to my advantage." The apostle Paul says, "All things work together for good to those who love God" (Rom. 8:28 NKJV). He did not say some things, but *all things*. They may not be good at the time we go through them. It's painful to go through a loss. It hurts when people do us wrong. It's discouraging when a dream doesn't work out. By themselves, they may not be good, but God promises He's going to bring it all together. One day you'll look back and say that it was all good.

We celebrate Good Friday each year. We call it "good" now, but two thousand years ago, on the day when Jesus was crucified, the disciples thought it was the worst day of their lives. Their dreams were shattered. The Man Whom they had devoted their lives to had been crucified, was dead, and had been buried in a tomb. *Good* is the last word they would have used to describe that Friday. *Tragic Friday, betrayed Friday, lonely Friday* would have seemed like more accurate descriptions.

When you're in the heat of the battle, it's easy to get discouraged. The disciples could have said, "God, why did You abandon Jesus in His time of greatest need?" But a few days later, when Jesus rose from the dead, they realized that He was Who He'd said He was. He had done what He'd said He was going to do. He'd defeated the enemy and brought salvation to mankind. They looked back on that Friday and said, "It wasn't what we thought. It was all a part of His plan. It was Good Friday."

What am I saying? It's all good. It may not be good right now, and it may not make sense on its own, but God knows how to bring it all together. If you'll stay in faith, one day you'll look back and say it was good.

>> Consider This <<

Isolate a significant incident in your past that you would say at
the time it happened was not good. Have you seen God bring
it all together and work good out of it? Describe how that
happened or what you're hoping will happen.

The steps of a *good* man are ordered by the LORD.

Psalm 37:23 NKJV

"You intended to harm me, but God intended it for good to accomplish what is now being done, the saving of many lives."

Genesis 50:20 NIV

>> Thoughts for Today <<

God is wonderful in His design and excellent in His working.
Believer, God overrules all things for your good. The needs-be for
all that you have suffered, has been most accurately determined by
God. Your course is all mapped out by your Lord. Nothing will
take Him by surprise, and there is nothing for which He has not
provided. He has arranged all, and you have but to patiently wait,
and you shall sing a song of deliverance.

Charles Spurgeon

Real satisfaction comes not in understanding God's motives,
but in understanding His character, in trusting in His promises,
and in leaning on Him and resting in Him as the Sovereign
who knows what He is doing and does all things well.

Joni Eareckson Tada

God's ways are behind the scenes, but He moves all
the scenes that He is behind.

John Nelson Darby

>> A Prayer for Today <<

Father, I trust You with all my heart. You know what's best for me. This is where You have me right now, and I believe that You are the One who orders my steps and that You hold me in the palms of Your hands. Even when I don't understand why a door remains closed or why a prayer is unanswered, I'm going to have a good attitude and be my best. I may not like it, it may feel bad, but I know a secret: it's all good. I believe that when it comes together, it's going to work for me and not against me. In Jesus' Name. Amen.

Takeaway Truth

You may have dreams that haven't worked out yet; you've had some disappointed Fridays. Don't get discouraged. Stay in faith. God knows what He's doing. If you'll keep honoring Him, being your best, then your Sunday is coming. You'll see your resurrection, so to speak. Sunday is when God vindicates you, heals you, promotes you, restores you, and opens doors that no man can shut. It's all good.

PERSEVERE
BELIEVE
GREATNESS
STRONG
BLESSED

CHARACTER
TRUST

CONFIDENCE
VICTORY
INCREASE

Nothing
Is Wasted

CHAPTER EIGHT

Key Truth

God has you in the palms of His hands.
Nothing that's happened to you has been
wasted. It's all a part of the plan to make you
into who you were created to be. It may not
have been good, but God can take the same
thing that should have destroyed you and use
it to propel you. No obstacle is too big,
no challenge too great.

Blessed
IN
THE DARKNESS

The main ingredient of the fertilizer we put on our flower beds at home is manure. It's waste, and it smells really bad for several days after we apply it. But in a month or two, the smell is gone and the plants are blossoming, filled out with lots of new growth from the manure's valuable nutrients and minerals that they could not get on their own.

In a similar way, we all go through things in life that stink. We don't like what someone did to us, or that a relationship didn't make it, or that we lost our main client, and it stinks. You need to have a new perspective: that's just fertilizer. It smells bad right now. You could easily be discouraged, but if you'll stay in faith, the stinky stuff—the betrayal, the disappointment, the loss—is getting you prepared for new growth, to bloom, to blossom, to become all you were created to be. It's not working against you; it's working for you. The truth is, you cannot reach your highest potential without fertilizer.

In the Scriptures, this is what Joseph did. His brothers were jealous of him and threw him into a pit. He could have gotten depressed and said, "God, I don't understand this. I'm a good person." Instead he realized, "It's just fertilizer. They're trying to stop me, but God's going to use it to increase me." However, that was just the beginning. His brothers sold him into slavery in Egypt, where his master's wife falsely accused him of a crime and had him thrown into prison. He spent thirteen years there for something he didn't do. They were trying to hold him down, but they didn't realize they were pouring fertilizer on him. Joseph kept growing, getting stronger, his roots going down deeper in faith.

All that injustice, that stinky stuff, seemed like a waste of years of his life, but that difficult, dark season was doing a work in Joseph, getting him prepared for the fullness of his destiny.

If you'll stay in faith in the stinky times, the times that don't make sense, when you're not treated fairly, when you're doing the right thing but the wrong things keep happening, your time will come to bloom, to be promoted, to be blessed, to be vindicated, and all the forces of darkness cannot stop you. People don't have the final say; God has the final say. He will get you to where you're supposed to be.

Joseph went from the pit to the prison and all the way to the palace. You may feel that you're in the pits right now. Perhaps you've had some bad breaks, you're dealing with a sickness, you've lost a loved one, a friend betrayed you, a dream died. But as was true of Joseph, that pit is not the end of your story, and the prison is not your final chapter. Your destiny is the palace. God destined you to live a victorious life. David said, "[God] also brought me up out of a horrible pit…has put a new song in my mouth" (Ps. 40:2–3 NKJV).

You may be in the pit, but you need to get ready, because you're coming out. Don't get comfortable in the pit. Don't let self-pity and discouragement steal your passion. You have to get your fire back. Every blessing that God promised you He still has every intention of bringing to pass. The palace is in your future. Victory is in your future. Dreams coming to pass are in your future, with increase, abundance, promotion, health, and restoration. That's what's up in front of you. That's where your story ends.

>> Consider This <<

Perhaps because of a mistake you made, a poor decision
that got you in trouble, the accuser whispers in your ear,
"You don't deserve to be blessed. It's your fault. God's not going
to help you." But God doesn't waste anything. He knows how
to get good out of every situation. What does the Samaritan
woman's story in John 4 tell you about how God can
use what you've been through?

....

....

....

....

....

....

....

....

....

....

....

....

....

....

....

....

....

....

>> **What the Scriptures Say** <<

Love bears all things [regardless of what comes], believes
all things [looking for the best in each one], hopes all
things [remaining steadfast during difficult times],
endures all things [without weakening].

1 Corinthians 13:7 AMP

When God made his promise to Abraham, he backed it to
the hilt, putting his own reputation on the line. He said,
"I promise that I'll bless you with everything I have—
bless and bless and bless!" Abraham stuck it out and got
everything that had been promised to him.

Hebrews 6:13–15 MSG

>> **Thoughts for Today** <<

You must learn, you must let God teach you, that the only
way to get rid of your past is to make a future out of it.
God will waste nothing.

Phillips Brooks

Nothing is ever wasted in the kingdom of God. Not one tear,
not all our pain, not the unanswered question or the seemingly
unanswered prayers. Nothing will be wasted if we are willing to
be patient until the grace of God is made manifest, and whether
it takes nine years or ninety, it will be worth the wait.

Author Unknown

No trials are wasted in God's economy.

Derek Prime and Alistair Begg

>> A Prayer for Today <<

Father in heaven, thank You that You know how to use what
I've been through and what I'm going through. You don't let
my experiences be wasted. I'm not going to let this stinky stuff
that I don't understand cause me to get sour and give up on my
dreams. I know it's just fertilizer. I believe that it's enriching me.
It's making me stronger. It's getting me prepared for new levels
and for something amazing in my future. I trust that You
will use me to help others who are going through
the same thing. In Jesus' Name. Amen.

Takeaway Truth

Nothing is wasted—the good, the bad, the painful. God knows how to bring blessing out of the dark places. He can take the broken pieces of your life—what seems like a waste and looks like nothing good will ever come out of it—and He knows how to make music out of your mess. If you'll stay in faith, not only will it act like fertilizer and help you, but down the road you'll be instrumental in helping others.

PERSEVERE
BELIEVE
GREATNESS
STRONG
BLESSED

CHARACTER
TRUST

JOY
CONFIDENCE
VICTORY
INCREASE

Trouble
Is
Transportation

CHAPTER NINE

Key Truth

You won't become all you were created to be
without trouble. Trouble develops something
in you that you can't get when it's easy
and everything is going your way. In the
difficult times and through every challenge
you've been through, you gain experience
that will transport you in the future.

. . . .

We all go through difficulties in life, but God uses troubles to move us toward our destiny. Nothing happens by accident. You may not understand it, but God wouldn't have allowed it if it weren't going to work to your advantage. Looking back over my life, I see the importance of the troubled times. It didn't make sense to me at the time, but years later I realized that if one door hadn't closed, a bigger door would never have opened. The challenges of the past prepared me for new challenges. I thought I was going backward, but God was setting me up to move forward. I didn't like it, I felt stuck, but the truth is that trouble was transportation; it was moving me into my destiny.

You don't grow in the good times; you grow in the tough times, the dark times. In the difficult times your spiritual muscles are developed, and you gain strength, endurance, and wisdom. Every challenge you've been through has deposited something in you; you gained experience that will help you in the future. The times when you failed, when you blew it, weren't wasted—you gained insight. It was all a part of God's plan.

Think about Moses. Pharaoh ordered the midwives to kill all the male Hebrew babies, threatening the life of the baby Moses (see Exod. 2). Some would say that it was too bad he was born at the wrong time. Hidden in a basket among the reeds along the bank of the Nile River, Moses' life could have ended by a thousand things, but none of it was a surprise to God. None of it cancelled Moses' purpose. God has the final say. People don't determine your destiny; God does.

Of all the people, Pharaoh's daughter, a princess, discovered the baby Moses and decided to take him as her own. And so Moses was raised in the palace of Pharaoh's daughter! God used the trouble to get Moses to where He wanted him to be. The trouble was a part of God's plan. If Moses had been raised in the limited environment he'd been born into, he could not have learned what he needed to for his destiny. In the palace, under the Pharaoh, he learned the best of Egyptian civilization—about business, leadership, how to conduct a meeting, how to speak to people, and on and on.

But at the time that Moses was taken away from his home and family, I'm sure that Moses' mother couldn't understand it. It seemed like a setback, but many years later, when God told Moses to go back to Egypt and tell the Pharaoh, "Let My people go," one of the reasons Moses could walk into Pharaoh's court with confidence was that he had lived in a palace and had been raised by Egyptian royalty. He wasn't overwhelmed.

What prepared Moses to lead the Israelites out of Egypt? Trouble. It was being born in a dysfunctional situation, having the odds stacked against him. If Pharaoh had not put out the decree, Moses would have grown up in his own home, but as a slave with a limited education. God knows what He's doing. You may not like the trouble, it may not be fair, you're uncomfortable, but that trouble is transportation. As it did for Moses, trouble is taking you to the next level of your destiny. It's getting you prepared. You wouldn't be who you are today without all the things you've been through.

>> Consider This <<

Exodus 13:17 says that God didn't lead the Israelites on the
easiest route to the Promised Land because they were not ready
for war. He had to toughen them up so they would be prepared
for what He had in store. What does that tell you
about the troubles you are facing?

>> **What the Scriptures Say** <<

God is our refuge and strength [mighty and impenetrable],
a very present *and* well-proved help in trouble.

Psalm 46:1 AMP

The LORD is close to the brokenhearted and saves those who are
crushed in spirit. The righteous person may have many troubles,
but the LORD delivers him from them all.

Psalm 34:18–19 NIV

....
....
....
....
....
....
....
....
....
....
....
....
....
....
....
....
....
....
....

>> **Thoughts for Today** <<

The little troubles and worries of life may be as stumbling
blocks in our way, or we may make them stepping-stones to a
nobler character and to heaven. Troubles are often the tools
by which God fashions us for better things.

Henry Ward Beecher

He who knows no hardships will know no hardihood.
He who faces no calamity will need no courage. Mysterious
though it is, the characteristics in human nature that we love
best grow in a soil with a strong mixture of troubles.

Harry Emerson Fosdick

God will not permit any troubles to come upon us,
unless He has a specific plan by which great blessing
can come out of the difficulty.

Peter Marshall

>> **A Prayer for Today** <<

Father, thank You for Your promise that You will deliver us
from trouble. You are the Most High God, the Creator of the
universe Who breathed life into me and crowned me with favor.
I trust You in trouble. I trust You when it's not happening my way.
I trust You even though I feel as though I'm going backward.
I believe that what I'm experiencing now is transporting me
to the next level of my destiny and I'm going to see You
connect the dots in my life and bring greater blessings
than I can imagine. In Jesus' Name. Amen.

Takeaway Truth

Shake off the discouragement. You may not understand what's happening, but God is in control. That trouble may look like a setback, but really it's a setup for God to do something greater. If you'll trust God in the trouble, that trouble is going to become transportation. God is going to open new doors, turn impossible situations around, and take you to the fullness of your destiny.

CHARACTER

TRUST

JOY

CONFIDENCE

VICTORY

INCREASE

PERSEVERE

BELIEVE

GREATNESS

STRONG

BLESSED

Dropped but Not Forgotten

CHAPTER TEN

Key Truth

We all get dropped in life—dropped by an
illness, by a divorce, by a friend who turns on you.
It's easy to feel alone and forgotten, as though
you don't matter. But don't get stuck in that
dark place. The God we serve is not only going
to lift you back up, but He's going to take you
to a higher place of blessing.

've learned you can't live very long without being dropped—dropped by a company layoff, by someone's rejection, by the loss of a loved one. Sometimes other people's poor choices have a negative effect on us. Maybe you were raised in an unhealthy environment, and now you're dealing with the same addictions, same depression, and same anger that surrounded you every day when you were a child. Some people were taken advantage of and mistreated; now they deal with shame and guilt, feeling as though they don't measure up. It wasn't their fault. Somebody dropped them. It's easy to get stuck in a dark place, thinking, *This is never going to change. It's my lot in life.*

You may have been dropped, but the good news is that our God knows how to pick us back up. David said, "[God] brought me up out of a horrible pit,…and set my feet upon a rock" (Ps. 40:2 NKJV). David was dropped by people coming against him, by rejection, by disappointments, and by his own failures, but God said, in effect, "Don't worry, David, that drop is not the end." In the same way, that bad break, that failure, those people who did you wrong, that sickness, that addiction, that chronic pain is not the end of your story.

If you've been dropped, you need to get ready. God is about to lift you and set you in a higher place. He's going to take you to a new level, to new opportunities, to new friendships, to new health, to new joy, to new fulfillment. You're not going to come out the same. The Scripture talks about how God will pay you back double for the unfair things that happened (see Isa. 61:7). Don't get discouraged or bitter. Get ready for double. Get ready for increase. Get ready for favor. Get ready for new levels.

God has not forgotten about you. He has seen every lonely night, every wrong that's been done, and every person who's ever harmed you. He's a God of justice. When the Israelites were being mistreated in slavery, taken advantage of by the Egyptians, He told them, "I'm coming down to make your wrongs right. I'm coming down to pick you back up. I'm coming down to bring justice, to deal with the people who have done you wrong." What causes God to get off the throne and take action is when He sees you being mistreated. When He sees that injustice, He doesn't sit back and say, "Too bad." He says, "That's My son, that's My daughter, My most prized possession. They've been dropped, and now I have to get down there to do something about it." When God goes to work, all the forces of darkness cannot stop Him. He'll make your wrongs right, He'll pay you back for the trouble, and He'll get you to where you're supposed to be.

If you feel alone and forgotten, don't believe those lies. God says, "See, I have engraved you on the palms of my hands" (Isa. 49:16 NIV). Every time God opens His hands, He's reminded of you. You may have had some bad breaks, some closed doors, some people who didn't do you right, but God hasn't forgotten about your dreams, He hasn't forgotten about the promises He's given you. Life happens to all of us, and you may get dropped, but remember that it's only temporary. God sees it. He's not only going to lift you back up, but you're going to come out better than you were before.

>> Consider This <<

Maybe you feel as though you've been dropped in a way similar
to Mephibosheth. Perhaps you had a bad break, lost a loved one,
or weren't treated right. What encouragement can you take
away from Mephibosheth's story? What happens when the
King summons you to the palace?

....

....

....

....

....

....

....

....

....

....

....

....

....

....

....

....

....

....

....

>> **What the Scriptures Say** <<

"Call to Me, and I will answer you, and show you great and mighty things, which you do not know."

Jeremiah 33:3 NKJV

But You, O LORD, are a shield for me, my glory and the One who lifts up my head. I cried to the LORD with my voice, and He heard me from His holy hill.

Psalm 3:3–4 NKJV

>> **Thoughts for Today** <<

Instead of concentrating on your problems and getting
discouraged, focus on God and meditate on His promises for you.
You may have fallen down, but you don't have to stay down.
God is ready, willing, and able to pick you up.

Joyce Meyer

When God lifts you up, Satan can never put you down.

Woodrow Kroll

Endurance is not just the ability to bear a hard thing,
but to turn it into glory.

William Barclay

>> **A Prayer for Today** <<

Father in heaven, I may have been dropped and had some
bad breaks, but that doesn't change the fact that I am Your child
with royal blood in my veins, and You are the glory and the
lifter of my head. I believe that just as You came down to make
things right for the Israelite slaves, You are coming down to make
things right for me. There is going to be a lifting out of the pit.
I believe that Your favor will open new doors, causing people
to be good to me, paying me back for what has been unfair.
In Jesus' Name. Amen.

Takeaway Truth

You may have been dropped, but God hasn't forgotten about you. You need to get ready, for your time is coming. Justice is coming, restoration is coming, promotion is coming, favor is coming, and new beginnings are coming. It's going to be far and beyond favor. You're not going to have to work for it. It will be the goodness of God, paying you back and bringing justice.

PERSEVERE
BELIEVE
GREATNESS
STRONG
BLESSED

CHARACTER
TRUST

JOY
CONFIDENCE
VICTORY
INCREASE

Balanced
Books

CHAPTER ELEVEN

Key Truth

God has promised that He will balance
the books of our lives. We all go through
unfair things that put us at a deficit. If nothing
changed, we would be out of balance. Life
is not always fair, but God is fair. He will add
up all the losses, the disappointments,
the heartaches, and the tears,
and He will pay you back.

Blessed
IN THE DARKNESS

. . . .

In accounting, the term *balancing the books* means making up for a loss. If an account has a deficit, when you balance the books, you have to first take all the losses and total them up. Then you know how much you need to add to balance it. One definition of *balancing the books* is "to equalize, to experience no loss." When the books are balanced, nobody can tell there's ever been a loss. There is no deficit.

In the same way, God has promised that He will balance the books of our lives. In Hebrews 10, the writer notes that the people had endured a severe time of suffering and persecution. He encourages them by saying that the time will come when they will be richly rewarded (see Heb. 10:35). He says, in essence, "God is a just God. He will repay the compensation owed us. He will settle the cases of His people." You may go through seasons when you're out of balance—you have a disappointment, a loss, something that doesn't make sense—but God is going to settle your case. He's added up every tear you've shed, every person who did you wrong, every injustice, every dark place. God is saying, "I'm about to balance your books." Compensation is coming, promotion is coming, vindication is coming, healing is coming, blessing is coming.

This is what happened with the Israelites. For 430 years the Israelites had been in slavery in Egypt. They were mistreated, taken advantage of, and forced to work long hours. In the Exodus, God was saying, "All right, it's time to balance the books." Just the fact that they were finally free to leave was a great miracle. But they didn't leave as broke, empty-handed slaves. They had worked all that time without being paid. On their way out, God caused them to have favor with the same people who had mistreated them. Suddenly their captors had a change of heart and gave them their gold, their silver, their jewels, and their clothing (see Exod. 12:13). That was God balancing the books.

God sees every wrong done to you and your family. As with the Israelites, there will be a time when He says, "Enough is enough." Isaiah 61:7 (MSG) says, "Because you got a double dose of trouble…, your inheritance in the land will be doubled and your joy go on forever." Don't complain about the trouble; that difficulty set you up for double. That bad break and disappointment may look like a setback, but God is about to balance the books.

Part of God's balancing your books is that people who didn't respect you, who dismissed you, and who discredited you are going to have a change of heart and ask for your blessing as Pharaoh did toward Moses (see Exod. 12:32). They're going to recognize the favor on your life. The Scripture says, "The king's heart is a stream of water in the hand of the LORD; he turns it wherever he will" (Prov. 21:1 ESV). God knows how to change people. You don't have to play up to them, or try to convince them to like you, or let them control and manipulate you in order to try to win their favor. No, walk in your anointing. Run your own race, always honoring God with excellence and integrity. God will turn the hearts of those who are against you. It may not happen overnight. It may take years, but God will balance your books.

>> Consider This <<

In the Scripture, a man named Saul was the biggest persecutor
of the early church (see Acts 9). Yet when Saul was at the point
of his deepest need, God sent a Christian named Ananias to pray
for Saul and speak to his need. How should you treat the Sauls
in your life, those who have been condescending toward you
and treated you as though you are less than?

....

....

....

....

....

....

....

....

....

....

....

....

....

....

....

....

....

....

>> **What the Scriptures Say** <<

When GOD approves of your life, even your enemies will
end up shaking your hand.

Proverbs 16:7 MSG

For God is not unjust. He will not forget how hard you have
worked for him and how you have shown your love to him
by caring for other believers, as you still do.

Hebrews 6:10 NLT

>> **Thoughts for Today** <<

If you have been mistreated, cheated, or deceived, and if your heart has been right all along, be assured that God knows this. God will eventually vindicate you, but in the meantime you should be confidently aware that God knows the truth concerning what has happened to you.

Theodore Epp

When God balances the scales morally, it is not some standard outside Himself He looks at and then determines whether this is right or wrong. But rather it's His very nature, it is His very character and nature that is the standard by which He judges.

Josh McDowell

Those blessings are sweetest that are won with prayers and worn with thanks.

Thomas Goodwin

>> A Prayer for Today <<

Father, thank You that You are the God of justice. You have seen the hurts in my life, and You feel my pain. I may be unbalanced right now, the discouragement may be heavy, but thank You that You're balancing my books. You know exactly what's going on, and You're not going to leave me in a place of deficit. You already have a way to settle my case and make things happen that I could never make happen. Lord, I believe payback is coming, restoration is coming, healing is coming. In Jesus' Name. Amen.

Takeaway Truth

You may have had some bad breaks, gone through things you don't understand. Take heart. The God of justice sees every injustice, every negative word, and He's adding up all the deficits, all the wrongs. At the right time, He will balance your books. Wait for God to do it His way. He's going to turn the darkest of situations around. Promotion is coming, vindication is coming.

CONFIDENCE
VICTORY
INCREASE

CHARACTER
TRUST

PERSEVERE
BELIEVE
GREATNESS
STRONG
BLESSED

Faith for the Middle

CHAPTER TWELVE

Key Truth

It's easy to have faith at the start. When your
baby is born or you start a business, it's exciting.
It's also easy to have faith when you can see the
finish line, you've fought the good fight, and the
dream is in sight. The challenge is having faith
in the middle—when it's dark and difficult
and not happening as you thought.

God never promised that we would reach our destiny without opposition and disappointments. The Scripture says, "Do not think it strange concerning the fiery trial which is to try you" (1 Pet. 4:12 NKJV). That means don't get upset because somebody did you wrong or because the business slowed. God is still on the throne. Nothing that's happened to you has stopped His plan for your life. What He promised you, He still has every intention of bringing to pass. I know you can have faith at the start—that's easy. I know you can have faith at the end. My question is, will you have faith in the middle? Will you have faith when it feels as though you're going in the wrong direction, when every voice tells you to give up and says, "You must have heard God wrong." Don't believe those lies. It's all a part of the process.

When God puts a dream in your heart, He'll show you the end. He'll give you the promise, but He won't show you the middle. If He told us all it would take for it to come to pass, we would talk ourselves out of it. In the Scripture an angel appeared to a teenager named Mary. He said, "Mary, you are highly favored of God. You will have a baby without knowing a man, and He will be the Messiah, the Savior of the world." God showed her the end. She was going to be the mother of Christ. She would have honor and be respected and admired for generations to come. I'm sure Mary was excited. But I can hear Mary years later, saying, "God, You didn't tell me that having this baby was going to cause my fiancé to want to call off our engagement. You didn't tell me I would have to live on the run for two years, hiding my baby from King Herod. You didn't tell me my son would be mistreated, betrayed, and mocked. You didn't tell me I would watch Him be crucified and die a painful death."

What am I saying? God doesn't give us all the details. What you're going through may be difficult, it doesn't make sense. This is where your faith has to kick in. Are you going to give up and talk yourself out of it? Or are you going to do as Mary did and say, "God, I didn't understand how difficult this would be. But God, I know You're still on the throne, and it's not a surprise to You. I'm not going to live in discouragement, give up on my dreams, or quit believing. I'm going to have faith in the middle."

God says, "When you go through deep waters, I will be with you" (Isa. 43:2 NLT). You may be in a flood, but He is saying, "You're not staying there. You're going through it." When you're in the middle, you need to remind yourself that this too shall pass. It's temporary. Now quit putting so much energy into that situation at work, being upset over that medical report, or being frustrated with that person who did you wrong. That's not your destination; you're only passing through. The trouble is not permanent. The sickness, the loneliness, or the difficulty is just a stop along the way. But if you give in to it and let it overwhelm you with discouragement, you'll settle there and let what should have been temporary become permanent. This is where many people miss it—they settle in the middle. I'm asking you to keep moving forward.

>> **Consider This** <<

When God brought the Israelites out of slavery, He showed
them their destination, the Promised Land, but not the details of
the challenges ahead. What are you in the middle of right now?
Is there a Red Sea in your path? In what way do you
need to exercise faith for the middle?

....

....

....

....

....

....

....

....

....

....

....

....

....

....

....

....

>> **What the Scriptures Say** <<

Though I am surrounded by troubles, you will bring me
safely through them…. Your power will save me.
The Lord will work out his plans for my life.

Psalm 138:7-8 TLB

For you have need of patient endurance [to bear up under
difficult circumstances without compromising], so that when
you have carried out the will of God, you may receive
and enjoy to the full what is promised.

Hebrews 10:36 AMP

>> Thoughts for Today <<

Perhaps you began to question God's love or His wisdom. Maybe you were afraid to say that He was wrong, but you sort of said, "God, You deceived me in letting me believe that this was the right thing to do. Why didn't You stop me?" A whole lot of wrong things can happen if you try to look at God from the middle of circumstances.

Henry Blackaby

The life of faith is not a life of mounting up with wings, but a life of walking and not fainting.... Faith never knows where it is being led, but it loves and knows the One who is leading.

Oswald Chambers

God never said that the journey would be easy, but He did say that the arrival would be worthwhile.

Max Lucado

>> A Prayer for Today <<

Father in heaven, I know that You are not just the God of the
beginning and the God of the end. You're the God of the middle.
You're the God Who will bring me through the trial, through the
adversity, through the loss, and work out Your plan for my life.
Thank You that I am not on my own and I'm not doing life on
my own. I believe that You will open doors that no man can
shut and turn situations around that look impossible. I have
faith for the middle. In Jesus' Name. Amen.

Takeaway Truth

God is not just the God of the start, not just the God of the finish; He's the God of the middle. Right now He's working out His plan for your life. Don't get discouraged by the process. You may be in the flood, but you're going to pass through it. If you'll have faith for the middle, the God of the middle will protect you, provide for you, and favor you. He'll take you into the fullness of your destiny.

CONFIDENCE
VICTORY
INCREASE

PERSEVERE
BELIEVE
GREATNESS
STRONG
BLESSED

CHARACTER
TRUST

Anchored
to Hope

CHAPTER THIRTEEN

Key Truth

The Scripture tells us that hope is the
anchor of our soul. When you are anchored
to this hope, nothing can move you because
you know God is still on the throne.
The winds, the waves, and the dark storms
of life may come, but you're not worried.
You have your anchor down.

T he Scripture tells us that "we have this hope as an anchor for the soul, firm and secure" (Heb. 6:19 NIV). What's going to keep your soul in the right place, what's going to cause you to overcome challenges and reach your dreams, is being anchored to hope. That means that no matter what you face, no matter how big the obstacle, no matter how long it's taking, you know God's plans for you are for good, that He's bigger than any obstacle, and that His favor is surrounding you. Nothing can move you from this hope.

But I've learned that there will always be something trying to get us to pull up our anchor—bad breaks, delays, disappointments. In these tough times, you have to make sure to keep your anchor down. If you pull it up, you'll drift over into doubt, discouragement, and self-pity. When you're anchored to hope, it's as though you're tied to it. You may have thoughts of doubt that say, "This problem is never going to work out." But your faith will kick in. "No, I know the answer is already on the way."

My question is, do you have your anchor down? Do you have that hope, that expectancy that your dreams are coming to pass, that you're going to break that addiction, that your family is going to be restored? Or have you pulled up your anchor, and now you've drifted into doubt, mediocrity, not expecting anything good? Put your anchor back down. Scripture says, "Faith is the substance of things hoped for" (Heb. 11:1 NKJV). You can't have faith if you don't first have hope.

One time David felt overwhelmed by life. He was down and discouraged and had given up on his dreams. He was stuck in a very dark place. But then he finally said, "Why are you cast down, O my soul?... Hope in God" (Ps. 42:5 NKJV). He realized that he'd let his circumstances cause him to pull up his anchor of hope. He said, in effect, "I'm going to put my anchor back down. I'm going to hope in the Lord."

You have to do as David did and hope in the Lord. Don't put your hope in your circumstances; they may not work out the way you want. Don't put your hope in people; they may let you down. Don't put your hope in your career; things may change. Put your hope in the God who spoke worlds into existence. When you have your hope in Him, the Scripture says you'll never be disappointed.

The prophet Zechariah said it this way: "Return to your fortress, you prisoners of hope;...I will restore twice as much to you" (Zech. 9:12 NIV). To be a "prisoner of hope" means you can't get away from it. You're anchored to it. You should be discouraged by everything that's come against you and overwhelmed by the size of the obstacles you're facing, but you know that if God is for you, none will dare be against you.

When you find yourself being consumed by worry, full of doubt, thinking it's never going to work out, recognize that you've pulled your anchor up. The good news is that you can put it back down and say, "Father, I thank You that the answer is on the way. Thank You that healing is coming, blessing is coming, freedom is coming, victory is coming." That's not just being positive; that's keeping your anchor down.

>> Consider This <<

If we don't keep our anchor down and stay full of hope, the
normal currents of life will cause us to drift. Little by little we start
getting negative and discouraged, and before we realize it, we're
in a dark place of doubt and worry and we've lost our passion.
Describe one area of your life where you've struggled with drifting.
What causes you to drift? Where does it take you?

>> **What the Scriptures Say** <<

Hope deferred makes the heart sick.

Proverbs 13:12 NIV

Through Him we also have access by faith into this [remarkable
state of] grace in which we [firmly and safely and securely]
stand. Let us rejoice in our hope *and* the confident assurance of
[experiencing and enjoying] the glory of [our great] God
[the manifestation of His excellence and power].

Romans 5:2 AMP

....

....

....

....

....

....

....

....

....

....

....

....

....

....

....

>> Thoughts for Today <<

Our hope is not hung upon such an untwisted thread as,
"I imagine so" or "It is likely," but the cable, the strong tow of
our fastened anchor, is the oath and promise of Him who is
eternal verity. Our salvation is fastened with God's own hand,
and with Christ's own strength, to the strong stake
of God's unchangeable nature.

Samuel Rutherford

Hope fills the afflicted soul with such inward joy and consolation
that it can laugh while tears are in the eye, sigh and sing all in
a breath; it is called "the rejoicing of hope."

William Gurnall

We must accept finite disappointment, but never lose
infinite hope.

Martin Luther King Jr.

>> **A Prayer for Today** <<

Father, thank You that in the midst of my difficulties, my hope can be anchored to You alone. I may not know how some negative circumstances can be changed or see how my dream can come to pass, but I know that You are fighting my battles. Thank You that behind the scenes You are arranging things in my favor. This is a new day, and I'm getting my hopes up. I'm cutting any lines tied to negativity and to living with no expectancy, and I'm anchoring myself to hope. In Jesus' Name. Amen.

Takeaway Truth

If you've become anchored to discouragement, worry, or negativity, you have to cut the line. God didn't breathe His life into you, crown you with favor, and give you a royal robe so you could go around anchored to doubt, fear, and bitterness. God created you to be anchored to hope, to go out each day expecting His goodness, believing that the days ahead are better than the days behind.

CHARACTER
TRUST
JOY
CONFIDENCE
VICTORY
INCREASE

PERSEVERE
BELIEVE
GREATNESS
STRONG
BLESSED

Pushed into Your Purpose

CHAPTER FOURTEEN

Key Truth

Sometimes God will let us be uncomfortable for a dark, difficult period so He can bless us later on. He'll close a door or shake things up, but later on, He'll open a bigger door and take us to a new level of our destiny. God is not as concerned about our comfort as He is about our purpose. He's pushing us into our purpose.

Blessed
IN THE DARKNESS

W e don't always understand why certain things happen to us, but not every closed door is a bad thing. Not every time a person walks away from us is a tragedy. God knows we won't move forward without a push. When everything is going well, we're comfortable. We don't want to stretch, to find a new friend, to develop new skills. To step out into the unknown can be scary. But if God had not shut that door, we would have been satisfied to stay where we were. God loves you too much to let you miss your destiny. You have too much potential, too much talent, too much in you for you to get stuck where you are.

None of the difficulties you've gone through, the bad breaks you've experienced, and the times when someone hurt you were meant to stop you. They were meant to push you, to stretch you, to mature you, to make you stronger. They deposited something inside you and prepared you for the new levels. It's made you into who you are today. When you face a difficulty, instead of being discouraged, instead of complaining, have a new perspective. *This is not here to defeat me; it's here to promote me. I may be uncomfortable, but I know that God is using it to push me to a new level of my purpose.*

When God told the prophet Samuel that He was going to take the throne away from King Saul because of disobedience, Samuel was so discouraged that God finally had to say to him, "How long will you mourn for Saul, since I have rejected him…?" (1 Sam. 16:1 NIV). God told Samuel, "I've found a new man named David, and I want you to go anoint him as the next king."

Notice the principle: if you'll quit being discouraged over who left, the right people will show up.

For seventeen years I loved doing the television production in our church. I thought that was how I would spend the rest of my life. But when my father went to be with the Lord, I knew that I was supposed to pastor the church. But I didn't think I could do it. I didn't have the training or the experience. My father had tried to get me up in front for years, but I was comfortable behind the scenes and didn't have to stretch. That loss pushed me out of my comfort zone, pushed me to discover new talents and into greater influence. Every time I've seen major growth in my life and stepped up to a new level, it happened because I was pushed. It involved adversity, loss, and disappointment.

You may be in a situation where you could easily be discouraged—you lost a loved one, you went through a breakup, your business didn't work out. The enemy may have meant that for harm, but God is going to use that to your advantage. Shake off the self-pity and get ready for new doors to open, for new opportunities, new skills, new friendships. Moses said, "As an eagle stirs up its nest, so God will stir up His children" (see Deut. 32:11). When things are stirring in your life, when things are uncomfortable—a door closes, a friend betrays you— don't think, *Well, that's just my luck. I never get any good breaks.* Turn it around and say, "God, I know You're in control and You're stirring up things because You're about to open new doors, You're about to take me to a higher level, You're about to push me into my purpose."

>> Consider This <<

Sometimes God moves people out of our life because He knows they will become a crutch and keep us from our potential. He'll cause a situation to dry up, so we'll be forced to change. Describe a situation where God led you to step into the unknown and take new steps of faith. Why was it so challenging? How did it change you and help push you into your purpose?

>> **What the Scriptures Say** <<

The LORD Almighty has sworn, "Surely, as I have planned,
so it will be, and as I have purposed, so it will happen."

Isaiah 14:24 NIV

Many are the plans in a person's heart, but it is the LORD's
purpose that prevails.

Proverbs 19:21 NIV

....
....
....
....
....
....
....
....
....
....
....
....
....
....
....
....
....
....
....
....

>> Thoughts for Today <<

A saint's life is in the hands of God as a bow and arrow in the hands of an archer. God is aiming at something the saint cannot see; He stretches and strains, and every now and again the saint says, "I cannot stand any more." But God does not heed; He goes on stretching until His purpose is in sight, then He lets fly.

Oswald Chambers

Don't bear trouble, use it. Take whatever happens—justice and injustice, pleasure and pain, compliment and criticism—take it up into the purpose of your life and make something out of it. Turn it into a testimony. Don't explain evil, exploit evil; make it serve you....take whatever happens and make something out of it.

E. Stanley Jones

Life's trials are not easy. But in God's will, each has a purpose. Often He uses them to enlarge you.

Warren Wiersbe

>> A Prayer for Today <<

Father in heaven, thank You that You use the winds that were
meant to harm me to push me into my destiny. You know
what's best for me, and You're pushing me for a reason. That
storm I'm facing is not going to defeat me; it's going to promote
me. You have something greater in my future, something bigger,
something better, something more rewarding up in front of me.
I believe that I'm about to tap into gifts and talents that I
didn't know I have. Thank You for stretching and
enlarging me. In Jesus' Name. Amen.

Takeaway Truth

Every storm and every dark, lonely season you've gone through pushed you to mature, to trust God in a greater way, to be more resilient and determined. Perhaps you're being squeezed, pressured, and it feels uncomfortable right now. If you'll keep the right attitude, God is about to push you to a new level. He's going to push you into greater influence, greater strength, greater resources.

PERSEV...
BELIEVE
GREA...RS
STRONG
BLESSED

CHARACTER
TRUST

CONFIDENCE
VICTORY
INCREASE

Step into the Unknown

CHAPTER FIFTEEN

Key Truth

Before you were formed in your mother's womb, God laid out your life plan. But He doesn't show you the details of how you'll get there. He leads you one step at a time. If you'll trust Him and take that step into the unknown, He'll show you another step. Step-by-step, He'll lead you into your destiny.

S imilar to a navigation system, God has a route overview
for your life. He not only knows your final destination,
He knows the best way to get you there. But God doesn't
show you the route overview. He doesn't tell you how it's going to
happen, how long it's going to take, or where the funds are going
to come from. He doesn't give you a blueprint for your whole life.
If you had all the facts, you wouldn't need any faith. He's going to
send you out not knowing everything. If you'll have the courage
to step into the unknown and do what you know He's asking you
to do, doors will open that you could never have opened, the right
people will show up, you'll have the resources you need.

The Scripture says, "Your word is a lamp to my feet, a light
on my path" (Ps. 119:105 NIV). "A lamp" implies you have
enough light to see right in front of you. He's not giving you the
light that shows your life for the next fifty years. It's more like
the headlights of a car. When you're driving at night, with your
low beam headlights you can only see a hundred feet or so in
front of you. You don't stop driving because you can't see your
destination, which is twenty-five miles ahead. You just keep
going, seeing as much as the lights allow, knowing you'll
eventually arrive at your destination.

My question is, will you take the next step that God gives
you with the light you have? If you're waiting for all the details,
you'll be waiting your whole life. We all want to be comfortable,
but walking in God's perfect will is going to make you a little
uncomfortable. You're not going to be sure how it's all going to
work out, but that's when you'll learn to trust God in a greater

way. God is not interested only in the destination. He's teaching you along the way; He's getting you prepared and growing you up. He will lead you purposefully into situations where you're in over your head, your friends can't help you, and you don't have the experience you think you need. God knew that you would be nervous, and He knew that you would feel unqualified. That's a test.

This is what Abraham did. God told him to leave the place where he was living and go to a land He would show him. Abraham was to pack up his household, leave his extended family behind, and head out to a land that God was going to give him as his inheritance. The only problem was that God didn't give him any details. The Scripture says, "He went out, not knowing where he was going" (Heb. 11:8 NKJV). I can imagine his wife, Sarah, asking, "Are you sure that God told you this?"

Are you going to talk yourself out of it? Are you going to let the fear of what you can't see hold you back? Or are you going to be bold and step into the unknown? The unknown is where miracles happen. The unknown is where you discover abilities that you never knew you had. The unknown is where you'll accomplish more than you ever dreamed. Just because you don't have the details doesn't mean God doesn't have the details. He has the route overview for your whole life. He wouldn't be leading you there if He didn't have a purpose. He has the provision, He has the favor, and He has what you need to go to the next level.

>> Consider This <<

When Jesus came walking across the stormy sea in the darkness of night, Peter was the only disciple who had the courage to get out of the boat and walk on the water to Him. How has being comfortable kept you from stepping into the unknown and becoming who you were created to be?

....

....

....

....

....

....

....

....

....

....

....

....

....

....

....

....

....

....

....

>> **What the Scriptures Say** <<

"I will lead the blind by ways they have not known, along unfamiliar paths I will guide them; I will turn the darkness into light before them and make the rough places smooth. These are the things I will do; I will not forsake them."

Isaiah 42:16 NIV

"Have I not commanded you? Be strong and courageous. Do not be afraid; do not be discouraged, for the LORD your God will be with you wherever you go."

Joshua 1:9 NIV

>> Thoughts for Today <<

It is not darkness you are going to, for God is light. It is not
lonely, for Christ is with you. It is not unknown country,
for Christ is there.

Charles Kingsley

As you walk through the valley of the unknown, you will find
the footprints of Jesus both in front of you and beside you.

Charles Stanley

We have ample evidence that the Lord is able to guide.
The promises cover every imaginable situation. All we
need to do is to take the hand He stretches out.

Elisabeth Elliot

>> **A Prayer for Today** <<

Father, thank You that You purposefully put me in situations where I don't see how things can work out and I can't do it on my own. When things look impossible, when I don't know where the funds are coming from, when every thought tells me to play it safe, I know that You want me to be bold, to take that step of faith into the unknown, and do what You've put in my heart. I believe that when I do, along the way I'll see miracles, doors will open that I couldn't open, and the right people will show up. In Jesus' Name. Amen.

Takeaway Truth

What God has in store for you is going to boggle your mind—the places He's going to take you, the people you're going to influence, the dreams you're going to accomplish. You know where it is—it's in the unknown, in what you can't see right now, in what you don't feel qualified for, in what looks way over your head. To reach your highest potential, have the boldness to step into the unknown.

PERSEVERE
BELIEVE
GREATNESS
STRONG
BLESSED

CHARACTER
TRUST

JOY
CONFIDENCE
VICTORY
INCREASE

I'm Still Standing

CHAPTER SIXTEEN

Key Truth

The Scripture says, "Rain falls on the just and on the unjust." Being a person of faith doesn't exempt you from difficulties. But when you live a life that honors God, when you build your house on the rock, and the storms of life come, when it's all said and done, you'll still be standing.

J esus told a parable about a wise man who built his house on a rock. This man honored God. Another man foolishly built his house on the sand. He didn't honor God. Then the rain descended, the floods came, and the winds blew and beat on the houses. What's interesting is that the same storm came to both people, the just and the unjust. If the story stopped there, you'd think that it doesn't make a difference whether we honor God or not.

Jesus went on to tell that after the storm was over, the house built on the rock was still standing. The house built on the sand was completely ruined. The difference is that when you honor God, the storms may come, but you have a promise that when it's all said and done, you'll still be standing. In tough times you have to remind yourself, "This is not the end. My house is built on the rock. The enemy doesn't have the final say; God does, and He says that when it's all over, I'll still be standing." You may suffer a setback and have to go through some dark, stormy times, but don't get discouraged or bitter—that's just a part of life. It rains on everybody. If you'll stay in faith, you have God's promise that when the smoke clears, when the dust settles, you'll be the victor. You'll still be standing.

We had a hurricane in Houston a few years ago. Huge sturdy oaks were no match for the winds. Pine trees over a hundred feet tall were lying in yard after yard. There was only one type of tree that I noticed wasn't blown down—the palm tree. It's because God designed the palm tree to withstand the storms. Unlike most other trees, the palm tree is able to bend so it will not break.

A certain kind of palm can bend over until the top is almost touching the ground, but when the wind subsides, it stands right back up as it did before. Why is that? God put bounce-back in the palm tree.

The Scripture says, "The righteous will flourish like a palm tree" (Ps. 92:12 NIV). It could have said that we'd flourish like a big, strong oak tree or like a tall, impressive pine tree. The reason God said we'd flourish like a palm tree is that God knew we would go through difficult times. He knew things would try to push us down and keep us from our destiny, so He said, "I'm going to make you like a palm tree with bounce-back in your spirit. You may go through a dark period of loneliness, of loss, of disappointment. The rain will come, but it's only temporary. You may be bent over right now, you may have some difficulties, but when the storm is over, you'll still be standing.

What's interesting is that when the palm tree is bent over during the hurricane, research shows that it's strengthening the root system and giving it new opportunities for growth. After the storm, when the palm tree straightens back up, it's actually stronger than it was before. When you come out of the storm, when you straighten back up, you're not going to be the same. You're going to be stronger, healthier, wiser, better off, and ready for new growth. God never brings you out the same. He makes the enemy pay for bringing the times of darkness and trouble. What's meant for your harm He's going to use to your advantage. It's not going to break you; it's going to strengthen you. You're not only going to still be standing; you're going to be standing stronger.

>> Consider This <<

When David suffered his greatest defeat and was deeply distressed, the Scripture says, "David felt strengthened and encouraged in the LORD his God" (1 Sam. 30:6 AMP). In your own words, how would you encourage yourself in the Lord? How do you stand up to the enemy and go after what belongs to you?

>> **What the Scriptures Say** <<

When the enemy comes in like a flood, the Spirit of the LORD
will lift up a standard against him.

Isaiah 59:19 NKJV

"Therefore whoever hears these sayings of Mine, and does
them, I will liken him to a wise man who built his house on the
rock: and the rain descended, the floods came, and the winds
blew and beat on that house; and it did not fall, for it
was founded on the rock."

Matthew 7:24–25 NKJV

....

....

....

....

....

....

....

....

....

....

....

....

....

....

....

....

>> Thoughts for Today <<

At the timberline where the storms strike with the most fury,
the sturdiest trees are found.

Hudson Taylor

Jesus is no security against life's storms, but He is
perfect security in them.

Author Unknown

Storms make the oak grow deeper roots.

George Herbert

>> **A Prayer for Today** <<

Father in heaven, thank You that my house can be built on the
rock that You are and that I can live to honor You. Thank You
for Your promise that no matter what comes my way, when the
storm is over, when the trouble passes, when the opposition ceases,
one thing I can count on is that I'll still be standing as a victor.
I believe that in the dark times, I am not alone. You are
fighting for me. You have brought me through in the past,
and thank You that You're going to bring me through
in the future. In Jesus' Name. Amen.

Takeaway Truth

You may be down right now, those winds are blowing, but like that bent-over palm tree, you're about to come back up again, better off—stronger, healthier, and promoted. This is a new day. Things are changing in your favor. You need to get ready, there's a bounce-back coming. Those winds can't topple you. When the dark storm passes, you'll still be standing, not the victim but the victor!

Remember
Your
Dream

CHAPTER SEVENTEEN

Key Truth

The Scripture calls your dreams "the secret
petitions of your heart." We feel them strongly and
know they're a part of our destiny. Life has a way
of pushing our dreams down, but God is saying,
"What I've promised you, I'm still going to do.
I spoke it and put it in your heart. I am true
to My word. It's on the way."

Blessed
IN
THE DARKNESS

All of us have dreams we're believing for, things we want to accomplish, but life has a way of burying our dreams under discouragement, past mistakes, rejection, divorce, failure, and negative voices. It's easy to settle for mediocrity when we have all this potential buried inside. But just because you gave up doesn't mean God gave up. Your dream may be buried in a dark place, but it's not too late to see it come to pass.

When God breathed His life into you, He put in you everything you need to fulfill your destiny. People can't stop you, and neither can bad breaks, disappointments, or loss. The Most High God is on your side. You have royal blood flowing through your veins. There are dreams in you so big that you can't accomplish them on your own. It's going to take you connecting with your Creator, believing that you're a person of destiny, knowing that God is directing your steps. You can still accomplish your buried dreams. Every time you remember your dream, every time you say, "Lord, thank You for bringing it to pass," you're removing some dirt. You're digging it out.

In the Scripture, this is what Caleb did. God put a dream into Caleb's heart for the people of Israel to go into the Promised Land at once, but his dream was buried because the other people believed a negative report. The Israelites were camped next door to the Promised Land, but they turned around, and that group of people never went in. I can imagine Caleb was discouraged. It looked as though the other people had kept him from his destiny. Most people would have given up and settled where they were, but not Caleb. The true mark of a champion is that even when some dirt gets thrown on a dream, they keep looking for new ways to move forward, believing for new opportunities.

Forty years later, when Caleb was eighty-five years old, he could still feel this dream stirring inside. At eighty-five Caleb went back to the same place where the others refused to go because giants lived there, and he said, "God, give me this mountain" (see Josh. 14:12). That's the dream that had been burning in him for all those years. He stirred it up and conquered the mountain that God had promised him. The dream came to pass.

Have you allowed any dreams to get buried in you? At one time you thought you could do something great—perhaps you thought you could lead a company or break an addiction—but that was a long time ago. You had some bad breaks that weren't your fault. You have a good excuse to settle; nobody would blame you if you did. But God sent me to light a fire inside you. That dream is still alive. You may have tried to make it happen a year ago, or five years ago, or forty years ago, but it didn't work out. Nobody helped you, and nobody encouraged you. God is saying to you what he said to Caleb: "Go back and try again. This is your time. Your destiny is calling out to you." You have to be like Caleb. Don't settle for less than your dream and refuse to enter the struggle. Your destiny is at stake! When you remember the dream, God will help you accomplish what you didn't accomplish early on. You can still become all you were created to be.

>> Consider This <<

What are the dreams that God has put in your heart? In the tough times when your dreams are not working out, what can you take from Joseph's story to help you endure?

>> **What the Scriptures Say** <<

Delight yourself also in the Lord, and He will give you the
desires *and* secret petitions of your heart. Commit your way to
the Lord [roll and repose each care of your load on Him];
trust (lean on, rely on, and be confident) also in Him
and He will bring it to pass.

Psalm 37:4–5 AMPC

But if I say, "I will not mention his word or speak anymore in
his name," his word is in my heart like a fire, a fire shut up in
my bones. I am weary of holding it in; indeed, I cannot.

Jeremiah 20:9 NIV

>> Thoughts for Today <<

The only place where your dream becomes impossible is
in your own thinking.

Robert H. Schuller

You are never too old to set another goal or to dream
a new dream.

C. S. Lewis

God gives us hopes and dreams for certain things to happen
in our lives, but He doesn't always allow us to see the
exact timing of His plan.

Joyce Meyer

>> **A Prayer for Today** <<

Father, thank You that You are the giver of all dreams. You are
the One who put the desires and secret petitions in my heart.
Search my heart and show me if there is anything that I've pushed
down, anything that I've given up on. Don't let me rest with any
dreams still buried. Thank You that bad breaks cannot cancel
my dreams and that the people who did me wrong or the
negative things that happened in the past are just additional
steps on the way to my destiny. I believe it's all a part of
the process. In Jesus' Name. Amen.

Takeaway Truth

You may have a dream that you've buried and given up on. You need to get your shovel out and start thanking God that it's coming to pass. It's easy to remember the hurt and the disappointment, but you must remember the dream, remember the promise. If you do this, the dreams you've buried will come back to life. You will rise higher, accomplish your goals, and become everything you were created to be.

PERSEVERE
BELIEVE
GREATNESS
STRONG
BLESSED

CHARACTER
TRUST

JOY
CONFIDENCE
VICTORY
INCREASE

An Expected End

CHAPTER EIGHTEEN

Key Truth

The prophet Isaiah said that God declares "the end from the beginning" (Isa. 46:10 NKJV). When God planned out your life, He started with where He wants you to end up, and then He worked backward. His plans for you are "to give you an expected end" (Jer. 29:11 KJV). Your end has already been established.

. . . .

This is what God has done for each one of us. When He planned out your life, somewhat like a movie writer does, He started with your final scene and then He worked backward. Here's the beauty of it. God's plans for you are "of peace, and not of evil, to give you an expected end" (Jer. 29:11 KJV). Your final scene has already been shot. The good news is that you don't end in defeat, in failure, in disappointment, or in heartache. You end in victory, as more than a conqueror, fulfilling your destiny. When you understand that your end has been established, you won't go through life upset because of a disappointment, frustrated because a dream hasn't come to pass, or bitter because of a loss. You'll stay in peace, knowing that in the end, it's all going to work to your advantage.

But here's the key: as in a movie, there will be twists and turns and scenes in your life that on their own don't make sense. If you stopped right there at the divorce, the sickness, or the loss, it would look as though things didn't work out. But what you don't realize is that's not your final scene. As long as you have breath, your movie is still in development. You may be in a difficult scene right now, and it may look as though a dream has died. You have to remind yourself that that's not how your story ends. You have an expected end. The Creator of the universe, the Most High God, has already planned it for good and not harm. If you'll keep moving forward, there's going to be another twist coming, but this time it will be a good break, a promotion, a restoration, a healing. God knows how to weave it all together. He's already established the end.

The Scripture says, "For the LORD of hosts has purposed, and who will annul it?" (Isa. 14:27 NKJV). This means that God has a purpose for your life. He's already planned out your days, lined up the different scenes, and established your ending. Then it asks, "Who will stop it?" God is saying, "I flung stars into space. I spoke worlds into existence. I'm the all-powerful Creator of the universe. Now, who can stop My plan for your life? Who can change your ending? People can't, unfair situations can't, tragedy can't. I have the final say." When you're on a detour, when you come to a dead end with something you don't understand, don't get upset or live frustrated. It's just one scene. When it all comes together, it's going to work out for your good.

The apostle Paul said that God will bring you "to a flourishing finish" (Phil. 1:6 MSG). He didn't say "to a defeated finish," "an unfair finish," "a lonely finish," or a "bankrupt finish." God has a victorious finish, an abundant finish, a fulfilled finish. When those thoughts tell you, "It's never going to work out. You have too many disadvantages. You're too far behind, and you've made too many mistakes," let those lies go in one ear and out the other. God has established the end, and He knows how to get you there. Now all through the day, just say, "Lord, I want to thank You that Your plans for me are for good. You've already shot my final scene. I may not understand everything along the way, and it may not have been fair, but I'm not going to live worried, upset, or discouraged. I know You're bringing me to a flourishing finish."

>> Consider This <<

God destined Joseph to become a leader in Egypt so he could help his family and the world in a time of widespread famine. That was the end. But his story took on several unusually dark twists. What was the real test of faith that Joseph faced...and we face? If Joseph were to talk with you today, what would he tell you?

>> **What the Scriptures Say** <<

Job answered GOD: "I'm convinced: You can do anything and everything. Nothing and no one can upset your plans."

Job 42:1–2 MSG

For the joy set before him [Jesus] endured the cross, scorning its shame, and sat down at the right hand of the throne of God.

Hebrews 12:2 NIV

>> Thoughts for Today <<

There is no greater discovery than seeing God as the author of your destiny.

Ravi Zacharias

Our yesterdays present irreparable things to us; it is true that we have lost opportunities which will never return, but God can transform this destructive anxiety into a constructive thoughtfulness for the future. Let the past sleep, but let it sleep on the bosom of Christ. Leave the Irreparable Past in His hands, and step out into the Irresistible Future with Him.

Oswald Chambers

The will of God is never exactly what you expect it to be. It may seem to be much worse, but in the end it's going to be a lot better and a lot bigger.

Elisabeth Elliot

>> **A Prayer for Today** <<

Father in heaven, thank You that in the midst of a very insecure world that I can rest in the security of knowing that my end has been set, knowing that I will have a flourishing finish, and knowing that You always cause me to triumph. I believe and declare that You are getting me prepared to be taken higher than I ever imagined and that all the forces of darkness cannot hold me down. All will end well for me. In Jesus' Name. Amen.

Takeaway Truth

When it feels as though you're far behind,
outnumbered, outsized, and outclassed,
instead of being discouraged, have a new
perspective. At any moment things are
going to shift in your favor—a good break,
a healing, or a promotion is coming. God has
the final say. He said, "I always cause you to
triumph." He didn't say "sometimes." He's
already shot your final scene. He's already
lined up the victory parade.